PETER GRILL AND THE PHILOSOPHER'S TIME

07

Story & Art by
DAISUKE HIYAMA

CONTENTS

Previously, on *Peter Grill*...

WELCOME...
TO THE ELVEN VILLAGE OF MINESTRONE...
CONSIDER IT AN HONOR!
YOU HAVE BEEN DEEMED AN HONORARY HIGH ELF, AND SELECTED...
AS PRIME BREEDING STOCK BY OUR SENATE FOR "PROJECT SUPER ELF"!
ARE YOU OFF YOUR TASTEFULLY CRAFTED ROCKER?
I'M A KIDNAP VICTIM OVER HERE!
WHAT PART OF THIS SCHEME SCREAMS OUT "I'MMA GO ALONG WITH THIS!"
COMPLIANCE IS APPRECIATED BUT NOT MANDATORY...
FSHHHHHH

WE WILL DRAIN YOU...
OF EVERY LAST DROP OF SAUSAGE SAUCE!
Chapter 29 Peter Grill and the Once-Noble House

YOU SEE, OUR GLORIOUS ELVEN VILLAGE...
HAS ALWAYS PERFORMED RATHER POORLY IN THE GRAND FIGHTING TOURNAMENT, WHICH VALUES COMBAT STRENGTH ABOVE ALL ELSE.
AS SUCH, IT HAS ALWAYS FOUND ITSELF VULNERABLE TO INVASION BY NEIGHBORING NATIONS, MAINLY OGRESTAN.
BUT AT LAST!!
OUR SENATE MADE THE DECISION TO SEEK OUT THE BLOOD OF TALENTED WARRIORS BEYOND OUR BORDERS!
WHY AM I GETTING A SENSE OF DÉJA-VU HERE?
GUESS THERE WAS SOME TRUTH BEHIND HER RAVINGS.
BUT THAT MAKES FIGURING OUT WHAT HER DEAL IS ALL THE HARDER!

USING THE BLOOD OF A STRONG, RENOWNED WARRIOR...
WE CAN REINFORCE OUR NATURALLY FEEBLE ELVEN BODIES TO RAISE THE PERFECT BATTLEMAGE WARRIORS...
THAT IS THE GOAL OF "PROJECT SUPER ELF"!
※ Artist conception, final product may differ.
ho
UPON APPROVAL BY THE SENATE, WE OF THE HOUSE OF ELDORIEL WERE NAMED SPECIAL GOODWILL AMBASSADORS!
ho ho!
oho
I, FULLTALIA ELDORIEL, AM HERE TO THOROUGHLY FULFILL MY DUTIES!
ho
ho
NOW THEN, PETER GRILL...
LIE BACK AND THINK OF PANNA COTTA!
HHHH!
AAH
WAH, STOP //////T...
WA
WHY DO YOU ELVES HAVE TO BE SO FORCEFUL ABOUT THIS?!
MAYBE A GUY LIKES TO BE ROMANCED, HUH? EVER THINK OF THAT?!

I DON'T UNDERSTAND.
A FILTHY HUMAN SUCH AS YOURSELF, BEING PRESENTED WITH TOP-SHELF ELF POON?
NATURALLY, YOU SHOULD BE JUMPING FOR JOY.
? ?
YOU ARROGANT LITTLE...!
SHE AND HER SISTER ARE LIKE TWO PEAS IN A POD!
※Her sister.
ANY-WAY!!
SHOOM
HOW MANY TIMES DO I HAVE TO TELL YOU ELVES THAT I'M NOT INTERESTED IN COOPERATING WITH YOUR PLANS IN THE SLIGHTEST?!
I'M GOING HOME BEFORE WE HAVE ANY MORE MISUNDER-STANDINGS!
TCH! YOU WRETCH...!
A MERE HUMAN REFUSING MY ELVEN DELIGHTS...?
I SHOULD HAVE WRECKED HIS HOME FOR GOOD MEASURE!
NO CHOICE THEN.
NOW THAT IT HAS COME TO THIS...

I'LL HAVE TO USE THAT!
THERE'S NO OTHER WAY!
TWITCH
HUH?!
IN THAT MO-MENT...
A NIGHT-MARE FLASHED THROUGH PETER'S BRAIN, CLEAR AS IF IT HAD BEEN YESTER-DAY.
I'VE GOT A...
THROBBING BONER...!
KUH... QUIT IT...
THERE'S NO NEED FOR CHANTING, HERE!
ENOUGH WITH THE WEIRD MAGIC, C'MON!
I'M BEGGIN' YA HERE!
HYAH!!
FLICK
FWSHOOOOOM
GHHAAA?!

WH... WHAT IS THIS...?!
AND WHAT'S WITH THE TRAMP STAMP ON MY STOMACH?!
OOOOOMM
WHAT HAVE YOU DONE...? WHAT DAMN ENCHANT-MENT HAVE YOU CAST ON ME THIS TIME?!
BEHOLD!
I SPENT QUITE A HEFTY SUM ON THIS MOST FORBIDDEN OF MAGICS, JUST TO CARRY OUT THIS MISSION!
NOW SUCCUMB TO OPERATION "TURN WHOLE BODY INTO AN EROGENOUS ZONE AND INCREASE TARGET'S SENSITIVITY THREE-THOUSAND-FOLD"!
BRAG!!
THAT'S PROFOUNDLY MORONIC...!

!!
ITCH...
AHH...
MY BODY...!
FIDGIT FIDGIT
MUH... MY BODY IS...!
RIIIIIISE
MY SENSITIVITY...!!
IT'S RISING!
OHOAA...
MUH... MY BODYYYY!
TWITCH TWITCH
OHO HO HO...
HOW ADOR-ABLE...
LOOK AT YOU... FLOPPING ABOUT LIKE A FISH ON LAND!

CELLOSE! GLUCOSE!
I THINK WE'RE *QUITE DONE* WITH THE FOREPLAY!
LET'S GET THIS STARTED, SHALL WE?!
GRAB
YOU GOT IT!
H-HEY! LEGGO!
WELL THEN, IT'S **FINALLY TIME.**
B-BMP
B-BMP
NOW TO PURGE YOU OF THESE GAUDY UNDER-GARMENTS AND...
GRAB
FREE YOUR SUBLIMELY STIFFENING SKY-SPLITTING STAFF!
LET IT BURST FORTH TOWARDS THE HEAVENS!
FWOOP!!
HUH...?!
THIS... CAN-NOT BE...?!

YOUR...
BUH...
RAMPAGING MASTODON IS A WOBBLY WORM?!
BWOMMMMMMP...
※The usual metaphor.
HOW IS THIS EVEN POSSIBLE?!
WHY AREN'T YOU ERECT?! CURSE YOU!
SMAK
AH!!
GHHAAHH!!
I-IT'S LIKE M-MY BODY...
I-IS SO SENSITIVE RIGHT NOW IT CAN'T EVEN THINK ABOUT DIVERTING BLOOD ANYWHERE!
MY LADY...
I BELIEVE THOSE UNDER THE ENCHANTMENT OF SENSITIVITY MAGIC NEED TIME TO ADJUST BEFORE THEY CAN GET RAGING HARD-ONS.
TCH...
NOW THAT YOU MENTION IT, THAT WAS IN THE INSTRUCTION MANUAL, WASN'T IT?

WELL, NEVER MIND!
WHAT WITH YOU BEING A WALKING ORGASM, YOUR ABILITY TO ESCAPE HAS BEEN GREATLY HAMPERED.
Oho ho ho!
I'LL TAKE MY TIME TWISTING YOU AROUND MY LITTLE FINGER! ALL IN DUE COURSE.
FULL-TALIA!
FLINCH
IS SOMEONE HERE?
GUG... GRAND-MOTHER!
FRAIL
FRAIL
Brassalia Eldoriel
High Elf (♀)
"Living on a pension."
PLEASE, GRAND-MOTHER!
YOU MUST GET YOUR REST...!
OH MY, WHY ARE YOU NAKED, CHILD?
AND WHAT OF THAT FELLOW OVER THERE...?

EHM, WELL YOU SEE...!! THAT MAN, HE'S...!!
A FRIEND...
HE'S A FRIEND OF MINE, YES!
PLAY ALONG IF YOU KNOW WHAT'S GOOD FOR YOU!
WAIT, WHAT...
I FEEL LIKE I'M MISSING SOME CONTEXT HERE!
OH MY, YOU ALMOST NEVER BRING FRIENDS HOME!
I'LL HAVE TO PREPARE SOME TREATS FOR OUR GUEST.
GRAND-MOTHER PLEASE, I APPRECIATE THE GESTURE, BUT...!
GRAND-MO-THER...!
IT ISN'T MUCH, BUT PLEASE ENJOY...
FTMp
THIS IS BASIC-ALLY JUST HOT WATER...
SIP SIP... SIP SIP...
I'M SO SORRY.
I WISH WE COULD OFFER YOU MORE.
TWITCH
TWITCH
※ As his body is 3,000 times more sensitive than usual, Peter Grill climaxes from simply feeling the tea slide down his throat.

HEY! ARE YOU JUST GONNA LEAVE MY BODY IN THIS STATE?!
O-OH... UMM... NOW'S NOT THE TIME TO TALK ABOUT THAT...
IT'S NOTHING, GRAND-MOTHER. PAY HIM NO MIND!
?
CARE FOR SOME SWEETS, YOUNG MAN?
N-NO...
WHY DO OLD PEOPLE ALWAYS OFFER YOU SWEETS ...?
STILL...
THIS PLACE IS HUGE, BUT LIKE...
IT'S IN A TOTAL STATE OF DISREPAIR. IF I DIDN'T KNOW BETTER, I'D SWEAR IT WAS ABANDONED.
YOU WERE JUST THINKING ABOUT HOW THIS PLACE IS IN DISREPAIR, AND LOOKS LIKE A RUN-DOWN MANSION, WEREN'T YOU?
C-CAN SHE READ MINDS?! RUDE, BY THE WAY!

BUT THERE'S NOTHING WE CAN DO ABOUT IT...!
WHAP
EVER SINCE THE INCIDENT BROUGHT UPON BY MY DARLING SISTER, OUR FAMILY HAS BEEN IN RUINS!
OUR COFFERS WERE EMPTIED FROM PAYING DAMAGES, AND OUR RELATIVES SCATTERED TO THE FOUR WINDS! ONLY GRAND-MOTHER AND I, AND OUR TWO SLAVES, REMAIN.
MY GRAND-MOTHER'S PENSION IS THE ONLY INCOME WE HAVE TO RELY ON...!
THIS MANSION IS ALL THAT REMAINS OF OUR FAMILY'S FOR-TUNE...
HOW CAN WE BE EXPECTED TO PROPERLY MAINTAIN IT?!
Main diet consists of plants they find lying around.
AND THIS IS MY PROB-LEM, *WHY?!*

SCREW YOU GUYS, I'M GOING HOME!
DASH!!
WAIT! I-I CAN'T JUST LET YOU LEAVE!
HYAH!!
BWOOOMFH!!
GUAAAAAHH!
※ The sound of erogenous sensitivity rocketing off the charts.
OH, I'M SO SORRY FOR THE TROUBLE.
IF ONLY MY HUSBAND WERE STILL HERE... FULLTALIA WOULDN'T HAVE TO GO THROUGH SO MUCH HARDSHIP...
GRAND-MOTH-ER...
HER GRANDMOTHER'S LAID-BACK TOO, HUH...
RUN AWAY AGAIN AND I'LL SEE TO IT YOU'LL NEVER FEEL SATISFACTION WITH YOUR REGULAR SENSITIVITY LEVEL EVER AGAIN, UNDER-STAND?
OKAY, OKAY!
I'LL BE A GOOD BOY FOR NOW!

HN...
COUGH ...!
GRAND-MO-THER...!
WE CAN'T HAVE YOU UP AND ABOUT LIKE THIS...
LET'S GET YOU BACK TO YOUR ROOM FOR YOUR MEDICINE, SHALL WE?
MAN...
TALK ABOUT CONFUSING.
JUST WHAT THE HECK...
IS HAPPENING HERE ANYWAY...?

Mean-while... A little earlier...
in Peter Grill's dorm house...
HEYYY!
PETER-SAMAAAA!
HAAH...
HAAH...
DID YOU FIND HIM?
NO.
PETER-SAMA IS STILL NOWHERE TO BE SEEN...!
HEY GUYS!!
I FOUND VEGAN TAKING A NAP OUT IN THE STREET!
TCH...
I REALLY DROPPED THE BALL THIS TIME.
TO LET THEM SNATCH PETER GRILL OUT FROM UNDER MY NOSE LIKE THAT...

WHAT HAPPENED, VEGAN-SAMA?!
THIS IS THE HANDI-WORK OF MY LITTLE SISTER.
I CAME HERE FROM THE ELF VILLAGE ON A MISSION TO GET PETER'S GUY GRAVY.
THAT IDIOT...
SHE NEVER LISTENS. NEVER DID...!
YOU MEAN TO SAY PETER-SAMA IS IN THE ELVEN VILLAGE...?
WELL, WHAT ARE WE CHATTING FOR?!
LET'S GO GET HIM BACK!
RIGHT ON!
THAT MEANS...
IT'S THE GRAND RETURN OF...
TEAM "LET'S GO SAVE SENPAI, AGAIN"!
TA DAAAA
※ The first mission to save senpai failed without even reaching its intended destination.

NO!
NOT THIS TIME!
THIS IS AN ELVEN VILLAGE PROB-LEM!
OTHER RACES ARE NOT TO MEDDLE IN OUR INTERNAL AFFAIRS!
I WILL TAKE RE-SPONSIBILITY FOR PETER GRILL'S SAFE RETURN!
THE REST OF YOU STAY HERE AND GORGE YOURSELVES ON CANDY OR WHATEVER, I DON'T CARE!
FARE-WELL!
SHA
AH!!
I-IS SHE GOING TO BE OKAY...?
ON HER OWN? MAYBE...
※ No faith in her whatsoever.
THOSE WERE SOME RIGHT PRETTY WORDS, BUT...
THERE'S A VERY REAL RISK THAT THE ELVES COULD GAIN EXCLUSIVE CONTROL OF PETER'S GUY GOODS!
WE'RE LEFT WITH NO CHOICE BUT TO INTERVENE!

YOU MEAN WE'RE GONNA DO WHAT WE CAN...
ON OUR OWN. RIGHT?!
YEAH... NO...
I AIN'T GOING.
BUT YOU GUYS HAVE FUN, 'KAY? GO *TEAM!* AN' STUFF.
AWW, DON'T BE LIKE THAT, MISSLIM.
WE ALL HAVE TO PITCH IN WHEN THE FAMILY'S IN TROUBLE!
GUHHH--
NYHHAAA?!
NYHAA!!
NUUUU! I DON WANNA-HAA-HAAAAAH!
I DON'T CARE ABOUT ANY OF *THIIIIIS!*
LET GO...
GO...
GO...
O...
※ 32 years old.

Our story now returns to the Elven Village.
Peter Grill has been imprisoned by the House of Eldoriel...
until such a time as his mind adjusts to its new three-thousandfold sensitivity.
His life there was tougher than he could've ever imagined!

MNNNN! ♡
The slightest breeze would throw him into fits of passion.
NH. ♡
Bathing became an orgy of delights...
Ascending to heaven every time food passed down his throat...
NH. ♡
He discovered strange new feelings excreting waste.
NH. ♡
Men's restroom
His newly heightened sensitivity caused such a strain on his everyday life...
ゼイ HAAH!
TH... THIS IS GOING TO KILL ME...
HAAH! ゼイ
that his dreams were all of flight. He hoped against hope that someday he might escape.

Until finally, one day...
THIS PAINTING...
IS THIS THE HOUSE OF ELDORIEL?
SO, VEGAN REALLY IS A PART OF THIS FAMILY...
NOW THAT BRINGS BACK MEMORIES.
YOU'RE...

IF I CLOSE MY EYES I CAN SEE IT AS CLEARLY AS IF IT WAS YESTERDAY.
THOSE SHINING HALCYON DAYS.
WHEN FULLTALIA-SAMA AND VEGAN-SAMA...
THOSE TWO SISTERS SURROUNDED BY THEIR WEALTHY FAMILY...
BOTH LIVED HAPPILY UNDER THIS ONE ROOF.
OH...
WE DOING A FLASH-BACK, HERE OR...?
I GUESS SO.

Three years ago...
YOU *IMPUDENT* LITTLE GNOME!
I'M GONNA LAND A DEVASTATING CORKSCREW BLOW RIGHT SQUARE IN THAT SMUG, SELF-SATISFIED GRIN OF YOURS!!
THAT PUDDING WAS MINE AND YOU KNOW IT!
HAVEN'T YOU LEARNED BY NOW THAT LITTLE SISTERS HAD BEST STAY OUT OF THEIR BIG SISTER'S HAIR?
YOUR APTITUDE FOR MAGIC IS ABOUT AS LOW AS YOUR INTELLIGENCE, AS EVIDENT FROM EVERY STUPID WORD THAT FALLS OUT OF YOUR MOUTH!
AGH! I'LL NOT ALLOW YOU TO BE-LITTLE MY GRACEFUL ATTEMPTS AT BE-COMING A PROPER LADY!
NOT TO MENTION HOW *AWFULLY* ARROGANT YOU'VE GOTTEN LATELY!
I'LL KILL YOU SO HARD *YOUR GHOST* WILL DIE!

死にさらせぇ
えええッ!!
THEN PERISH!!
VEGAN-SAMA WAS THE FINEST MAGIC USER IN THE VILLAGE...
AND FULLTALIA-SAMA WAS BLESSED WITH THE FINEST BODY.
THEY WERE BOTH RESPECTED AND ADMIRED BY ALL.
YOU SURE THEY WEREN'T MAKING SURE THEY DIDN'T BURN THE JOINT DOWN?
THAT IS... UN-TIL...
THE INCIDENT THAT RESULTED IN VEGAN-SAMA'S BANISHMENT FROM THE VILLAGE.
AND BROUGHT THE HOUSE OF ELDORIEL TO ITS KNEES WITH DEBT.
THE DREADED "MINE-STRONE IN THE PUDDING INCIDENT."
HOW'D IT GET A DUMB NAME LIKE THAT?

BY THE WAY...
VPP
ARE YOU BUSY RIGHT NOW?
HM?
THERE'S SOMEPLACE I NEED TO SHOW YOU.
WHU-DOOM
WHAZZIS ...?
A STORE-HOUSE?
IN DAYS PAST, WHEN THE ELDORI-ELS WERE LOADED...
THEIR GREAT-GREAT-GRANDFATHER VEGETALIA-SAMA LEFT THE SISTERS A BIRTHDAY PRESENT, LOCKED AWAY IN HERE.
MANY THINK IT WAS A "GREAT IN-HERITANCE" HE LEFT BEHIND.

When the powers of two sisters combine
this seal shall open
AS THE STORY GOES, THE DOOR SHALL ONLY OPEN ONCE THEY WORK TOGETHER AND POUR MAGIC INTO IT.
IT MUST'VE SADDENED HIM TO SEE HIS GRAND-DAUGHTERS AT EACH OTHER'S THROATS...
BUT IN THE END THEIR RELATIONSHIP JUST DETERIORATED FURTHER AND... THAT WAS THE END OF THAT.
WHAT A WASTE.
JUST BETWEEN YOU AND ME...

"SPECIAL GOOD-WILL AMBASSADOR."
THE TITLE SOUNDS NICE ON THE SURFACE...
BUT IT'S REALLY A DIRTY JOB THAT WAS PUSHED ON THE HOUSE OF ELDORIEL AS A MEANS TO PAY OFF DEBTS.
THEY NEVER INTENDED NOR WANTED TO HAVE THIS "HONOR" THRUST UPON THEM.
WELL... FIGURES...
ELVES LOOK DOWN ON THE OTHER RACES, THEY DON'T RESPECT THEM...
LET ALONE DESIRE TO BEAR THEIR CHILDREN.
YOU MEAN IF FULLTALIA AND VEGAN MADE UP, THEY'D GET WHATEVER INHERITANCE IS IN THIS STORE-HOUSE...?
YEAH...
OUR IMMEDIATE FINANCIAL PROBLEMS WOULD BE OVER...
AND THEY MIGHT EVEN BE FREED FROM THEIR ROLES AS AMBASSA-DORS.

WHY ARE YOU TELLING ME ALL THIS?
WELL...
I'M NOT EXACTLY ON THE BEST TERMS WITH VEGAN-SAMA, TO BE HONEST...
BUT YOU SEEM TO BE FRIENDLY WITH HER.
IT MIGHT BE RUDE OF ME TO EVEN SUGGEST THIS, BUT...
IF THERE'S ANY WAY YOU COULD BRING FULLTALIA-SAMA AND VEGAN-SAMA CLOSER TOGETHER...
GREAT! MAKE MY KIDNAPPER AND MY RAPIST GET ALONG, WHAT COULD GO WRONG?
HMM, SOUNDS LIKE THERE'S A HEAP OF BAGGAGE BETWEEN THOSE TWO.
AT THE END OF THE DAY...
BUT THE TRUTH IS...
NO WAY AM I TACKLING SUCH SERIOUS TOPICS...
WHEN MY BODY'S THREE THOUSAND-TIMES MORE SENSITIVE THAN NORMAL.
IN ONE EAR AND OUT THE OTHER.

I'M DREADFULLY SORRY, BUT COULD WE PLEASE...
REQUEST ANOTHER SMALL DEFER-MENT...?!
HUH?
THAT'S FULL-TALIA'S VOICE...
SHE SOUNDS UPSET...?
OF COURSE ...
YOU WOULD SAY THAT NOW!
WE WIPED THE HOUSE OF ELDORIEL'S DEBT FROM THE BOOKS IN EXCHANGE FOR THE POSITION OF "SPECIAL GOODWILL AMBASSADOR" WE ASSIGNED YOU, NO?
SO, JUST HOW LONG...
ARE WE TO BE MADE TO WAIT?!

OUR DIVINE PATIENCE AND GRACE HAS LIMITS, YOU KNOW?
Lazy Son of Some Senator
"I'm not even going to give him a name, that's how much of a minor character he is."
AN-OTHER SMALL DEFER-MENT, *PLEASE* ...!
WE HAVE ALREADY OBTAINED THE NECESSARY WARRIOR!
WELL, TO BE PER-FECTLY HON-EST...
I DIDN'T MUCH APPROVE OF ALLOWING A FILTHY HUMAN'S BLOOD TO POLLUTE OUR ILLUSTRIOUS VILLAGE'S GENE POOL.
BUT FOR PENNILESS BEGGARS SUCH AS YOUR-SELVES...
THIS ROLE SEEMS TO HAVE BEEN TAILOR-MADE FOR YOU.

KEEP YOUR COOL, MY LADY...
PLEASE, RESTRAIN YOUR-SELF...!
TREMBL TREMBL TREMBL
I'M WELL AWARE, DAMN YOU...
I'M PER-FECTLY CALM AND COLLEC-TED...!
IN ANY CASE!
THMP
WE'D LIKE TO SEE RESULTS SOONER RATHER THAN LATER!
WE'LL BE BACK TO CHECK ON YOU SOON.
YOU'LL HAVE GOOD NEWS FOR US BY THEN I TRUST, HM?
HEH HEH HEH!
ピキ ピキ
POP POP
ピキッ
POP

GRAAAGHH!!
HUMILIA-TED! HUMILIA-TED! HUMILIA-TED!
WHY MUST I KNEEL AND LISTEN TO THE LIKES OF THOSE CRETINOUS PIGS!
GRAAAHHH!
THOKK
MY LADY! PLEASE COMPOSE YOURSELF...!
AH!
PLEASE, RELAX...
DRINK SOME TEA! TAKE DEEP BREATHS...!
O-OF COURSE, NOW WHAT WAS I THINKING...
I LOST MY COMPSURE FOR A MOMENT THERE.
MY USUAL BLEND IS PERFECT FOR TIMES SUCH AS THESE!
SLRP
RIGHT THEN! I'M PERFECTLY CALM!
Basically just hot water.
GH...
GHH...
M-MY LADY...?
GHH!
PLIK
PLIK
NHHHHHH!

わあああああ
WAAAAAAHHN!
WAHHHHHH!
I HAA-AATE THIS!
ぼろ SOB
ぼろ SOB
I HATE THIS STUPID JOB THEY'RE MAKING ME DO...!
EVEN THE HUMAN LOOKS DOWN ON ME!
IT TOOK EVERY LAST PENNY WE HAD JUST TO BRING HIM BACK HERE...!
I GALLANTLY OFFERED HIM MY VIRTUE BUT HE TURNED ME DOWWW-WWWN!
HE DIDN'T EVEN POP A BONERR-RRR!!
......
AH, I CAN'T TAKE IT ANY MOOOO-OOORE!

I'M ALMOST...
BWAAAAH!
STARTING TO FEEL SORRY FOR HER.
UH...
COME ON PETER, WHAT ARE YOU THINKING?!
YOU DON'T NEED TO SYMPATHIZE WITH HER!
SHE KIDNAPPED YOU AND MADE YOU THREE THOUSAND TIMES MORE SENSITIVE THAN USUAL!
FTT
NH?
REMOVE YOUR GARMENTS, PETER GRILL.

GLARE
DID IT JUST GET COLD IN HERE?
DOOM DOOM DOOM DOOM DOOM
......
HUH?
RMB RMB RMB RMB RMB RMB RMB RMB
I SAID...
DISROBE IMMEDI-ATELY!
NOW THAT ANGER HAS THE BEST OF ME...
I NO LONGER HAVE ANY CHOICE IN HOW I PROCEED WITH THIS SITUATION!
?!

STAMP
MY LADY! ARE YOU REALLY GOING TO--
YES.
STOMP
STOMP
SURELY PETER GRILL'S MIND MUST HAVE ADJUSTED BY NOW!
I'M PUTTING AN END TO THIS FARCE!
HERE AND NOW!
HYAAH!!
WHOSHH

HUH?!
WHSHHH
WHAT'S GOING ON?!
FSHHHHH
WHAT IS THIS...?!
GLOOP
WHOOM!!
IS THIS...
AN ILLUSIONARY SPACE OR SOMETHING?!
GLOOP BLOOP

BUHBLOOP
BLUPP BLURP
HUH?!
TA-DAAAAA!!
L-LUVEL-LIA-SEN-PAI?!

WH-WHAT'S THE MEANING OF THIS?!
I THOUGHT FULLTALIA WAS MAKING HER BIG MOVE, BUT INSTEAD LUVELLIA-SENPAI'S HERE?!
THIS CAN'T BE REAL, CAN IT?!
B... BUT...! AHH...!
L-LUVELLIA-SENPAI'S BOOBS ARE...
SO TANTA-LIZINGLY WITHIN REACH...!
HMPH!
SO EASILY DE-CEIVED...
BEHOLD, THE HOUSE OF ELDORIEL'S FORBIDDEN ILLUSIONARY MAGIC...!
THIS MAN SHOULD BE SEEING ME AS HIS HEART'S TRUE DESIRE!
※ Back in reality.

MY PRIDE'S BEEN HOLDING ME BACK FROM USING THIS TILL NOW.
BUT THAT DOESN'T MATTER ANYMORE!
WHAT USE IS PRIDE IF IT COSTS ME RESULTS?!
GLARE
PETER-KUUUN...
I THINK I FIGURED OUT...
HOW BABIES GET MADE...!
※ Illusion
WH-
WAAHHHH!!
AH! NO, I CAN'T!
LUVELLIA-SENPAI, NO! DON'T DO IT, LUVELLIA-SENPAI!

W-WAKE UP... I HAFTA WAKE UP!
WAAAAH!!
YOU KNOW THE *REAL* LUVELLIA-SENPAI WOULD NEVER BE TALKIN' ABOUT MAKIN' BABIES!
YOU WANT TO GET CARRIED AWAY WORSE THAN EVER? BECAUSE *THIS* IS HOW IT HAPPENS!!
PSHT! WHO CARES ABOUT THAT! GET UP IN THERE, BRO!
FLINCH
FLINCH
YOU'RE THREE THOUSAND TIMES MORE SENSITIVE, HAVE YOU ANY IDEA HOW *AWESOME* THAT'S GONNA FEEL?!
NHH!
B-BMP
B-BMP
B-BMP
B-BMP
WH-WHO ARE THESE GUYS?
YOU KNOW WHAT THEY SAY...
WHAT HAPPENS IN THE ELVEN VILLAGE *STAYS* IN THE ELVEN VILLAGE...!
B-BMP
B-BMP
B-BMP
TRUU-UUST US...!
WE'RE THE CHEATING MASTERS!
※ The old angel and devil on your shoulders routine.

IF NO ONE FINDS OUT...
IS IT EVEN CHEATING AT ALL?!
Chapter 29 / END

Use the door, Peter...

PETER GRILL
AND THE PHILOSOPHER'S TIME

Previously, on *Peter Grill*...

IT DOESN'T MATTER...
SO LONG AS NO ONE FINDS OUT!
Chapter 30 Peter Grill and the Sisterly Feud

Z
Z
Z
IS HE ASLEEP OR SOMETHING?!
WHAT'S WITH THE EXCESSIVE SHOULDER DEVILS!
I NEED SOME MORAL GUIDANCE HERE! WHERE'S ANGEL-ME?!
PETER-KUUUU-UN...
COME.
LET'S MAKE THE BEAST WITH TWO BACKS... KAY?
UGHHGGH! I CAN'T LET THIS HAPPEN!
THERE HAS TO BE SOMETHING IN THIS HORRIBLE HAND I CAN USE!
AH!
IT WAS AS IF PETER GRILL HAD BEEN STRUCK BY A THUNDER-BOLT!
"HAND?!"

THAT'S IT...!
I JUST HAVE TO PLAY MY "HAND...!"
BUT THIS IS ALL JUST THEORETICAL.
CAN I REALLY PULL THAT OFF IN A SITUATION LIKE THIS?!
NO...!
BUT I... I HAVE TO...!
TO OVERCOME THIS, I...
I HAVE TO MAN UP AND JUST GO WITH IT!

OHO HO HO...
PAH-THETIC! IN THE END YOU REALLY ARE JUST SLAVE TO YOUR BASER INSTINCTS.
WITH THE LOVE OF HIS LIFE RIGHT BEFORE HIS EYES AND HIS SENSITIVITY BOOSTED TO HIGH HEAVEN...
BENEATH THAT FLIMSY UNDERGARMENT LURKS A SPICY SAUSAGE JUST BEGGING TO SERVE ITSELF TO ME!
GRAB
NOW!
THIS TIME FOR CER-TAIN...!
HERE, ALLOW ME TO FREE THAT SOLID STIFFY...
LET IT BURST FROM YOUR TROU-SERS!

HUH...?
H... HOW CAN THIS BE...?
パオオォ…
BWOOOOOMP...
YOU'RE SOFTER THAN A MARSH-MALLOW?!
IM-POSSIBLE! I... I WAS SURE I SAW...
※ You know the drill.
HUH?!
ドドドド
B-BMP B-BMP B-BMP B-BMP
ドドドド
B-BMP B-BMP B-BMP B-BMP B-BMP B-BMP

B-BMP
B-BMP
B-BMP
B-BMP
B-BMP
B-BMP
B-BMP
TH...
THAT FACE...!
THE PHILOSOPHER...!
THAT IS THE FACE OF A PHILOSOPHER!
It happened in a flash.

When Fulltalia purged Peter Grill's clothes from his body...
in that one moment...
he seized the opportunity.
Peter moved the strongest right arm on Earth...
and with speed...
which no mere mortal could perceive...
he went berserk.
And with his member, he played...

MACH SPEED FLESH FLUTE SALUTE!
WHSHHH
Only that sensitive body, reaching the peak of its raging tides...
coupled with the speed of the Strongest Man on Earth allowed this unique miracle to manifest!
WH...?!
I-INCON-CEIV-ABLE...!

HOW ON EARTH DID YOU RELIEVE YOURSELF LIKE THAT?!
AND WHYYYY-YYY?!
With this miracle having come to pass, Peter Grill came crashing down into his usual philosopher's time!
With his own hand, he had returned himself to a resting stance, and bought himself time until his next arrow could be fired.
BUUUCHHH...
TCH!
WHOOSH
THE ILLUSION IS FADING?!
INCREDIBLE...!
NEVER HAD I EXPECTED HE WOULD USE SUCH WRONG-HEADED TACTICS TO BREAK MY HOLD ON HIM...!

SO... IT WAS YOU IN FRONT OF ME ALL ALONG.
SIGH
THAT WAS A CLOSE CALL... UNFORTUNATELY FOR YOU!
WITH THIS TACTIC I CAN RETREAT FROM ANY ADVANCES YOU MAKE ON ME!
UNLESS YOU FREE ME FROM THIS SENSITIVE BODY, YOU'LL ONLY HAVE TWO OR THREE MORE PHILOSOPHER'S TIMES TO WAIT THROUGH!
WHY YOU IMPUDENT...
I WON'T LET IT END LIKE THIS, PETER GRILL!
GRAWWRR
I'LL CAST MY ILLUSION AGAIN AND...
FLAP FLAP FLAP
HM?
WH... WHAT'S THAT THING...?
Peter Grill...
In three seconds...
close your eyes!
HUH...?

FLASHH!!
NH!
I-IT'S SO BRIGHT!
N-NO..! HE'S GONE?!
WHERE'S HE RUN OFF TO?!
NOT FAR, FULL-TALIA.
FLINCH

BAM!!!
SUH... SISTER?!
OH, MY... DID I FORGET TO KNOCK?
WHAT ARE YOU EVEN DOING HERE, YOU CRETIN!
HAND HIM OVER!
HNNNNNGH!
GRR GRR
FULL-TALIA.
WHPP
IT'S PROBABLY BEST I MAKE IT CLEAR TO YOU HERE AND NOW...

PETER GRILL AND I ARE MADLY IN LOVE WITH EACH OTHER!
OUR SWEAT-COVERED BODIES HAVE INTERTWINED COUNTLESS TIMES, AND WE ARE RESOLVED TO WED FORTHWITH!
FUNNY...!
I DON'T RECALL ANY OF THIS?!
THE ROLE OF "SPECIAL GOODWILL AMBASSADOR" IS MINE BY RIGHT!
GIVE UP NOW AND SIT OVER THERE IN THE CORNER QUIETLY EATING WEEDS, OR WHATEVER IT IS YOU DO!
GHH...
YOU WERE BANISHED FROM THIS VILLAGE, AND YET YOU DARE TO SHOW YOUR FACE AND STAND IN MY WAY...?
AS EVER, YOU PROVE TO HAVE THE PERSONALITY OF BOILED DUNG SOUP, SISTER DEAR!

FULLTALIA, MY CHILD...
IS SOMETHING THE MATTER? I HEARD RAISED VOICES...
GUH...
GRAND-MOTH-ER...!
VEGAN?
VEGAN, IS THAT YOU...?!
GRAND-MOTHER...

I'LL RE-STORE THE HON-OR...
UNTIL THEN...
OF THE HOUSE OF ELDORIEL WITH MY OWN TWO HANDS.
STAY WELL, WON'T YOU...?
I WON'T LET YOU ESCAPE, SISTER DEAR!
HI-YAH!!
HI-YAH!!
TOO SLOW, NINCOM-POOP!
WHOOSHH!!
FLICK
AGHH!

NO, IT CAN'T BE...!
B-BMP
B-BMP
B-BMP
B-BMP
B-BMP
B-BMP
B-BMP
THIS MAGIC ...!
FUU
THAT'S FOR YESTER-DAY.
PRO TIP: YOU PROB-ABLY SHOULDN'T MOVE.
R-I-I-I-I-SE
MY SEN-SITIV-ITY...!
IT'S MOUNT-ING!
Nhhaah!
MUH... MY BODY!
MY LADY!
LET'S GO, PETER GRILL!
JUMP
UH...
AHHHN!
OKAY...!

MY LADY! WHAT SHOULD WE DO?!
TCH...
CELLOSE, GLUCOSE, BOTH OF YOU GIVE CHASE!
DO NOT LET THEM GET AWAY!
HFF!
HFF!
I WILL FULFILL MY ROLE AS THE SPECIAL GOODWILL AMBASSA-DOR...!

Mean-while...
KRA-KOOM
Let's check in on the other harem members, who were **supposed** to be saving the Strongest Man on Earth.
HAAH! HAAH!
IZZ SOOO FREAK-IN' HOOO-OT!
HAAH!
HEYYYY...
YOU SURE THIS IS THE WAY TO THE ELVEN VILLAGE?!
HMM...
LIKE... IT'S SUPER WEIRD... ACCORDING TO THE MAP IT SHOULD BE AROUND HERE SOME-WHERE?
E-EXCUSE ME...
MIMI-SAMA, THIS MIGHT BE IMPERTINENT OF ME TO SAY, BUT...
IT APPEARS THE MAP...
IS UPSIDE DOWN.
UH!!
OH YEAA-AAH!!

YOU ...!
FECK-LESS...!
HGAH!!
ARE YOU KIDDING ME HERE?!
YER SO DEAD!
SO, WE'VE BEEN GOING THE WRONG WAY THIS WHOLE TIME, HUH?
NOW, NOW... NO POINT IN GETTING ANGRY, MISSLIM.
IS THIS A BAD TIME TO MENTION THE ROAD HAS SEALED OFF BEHIND US?
GLOOP
GLOOP
GLOOP
WHAT-EVER SHOULD WE DO...?
AH!
MISSLIM, DON'T MOVE!
SHHHNK
NYAAAHHAAA?!

STARTING TO GET AWFUL MONSTER-Y AROUND HERE...
NO CHOICE BUT TO PRESS ON.
FLAP
FLAP
"Tryhard Handsome Guy" Monsters
Capture difficulty level 64
YEAH...
AND HERE I THOUGHT THINGS'D GET DULL!
※ No remorse.
As usual, their journey was a cheerful, random wander.
WRROOAAR
And though I do digress...
while fighting back the monsters from their path, their chests bounced furiously...
and the resulting vibrations created a wind that imperceptibly altered the structure of the world around them...

Those vibrations traveled throughout the world, rippling out and disrupting the fated order of things.
Ultimately, the ripples found their way to the Elven Village, where they would set important events in motion...
But at the time...
they themselves had no way of knowing what they had done.
Our story returns once more to the Elven Village of Minestrone.

THEY'RE GONE...
THE WHOLE TOWN'S CRAWLING WITH SOLDIERS.
EVERY TIME THEY SEE YOU, THEY WINCE AND START CHASING US. WHAT DID YOU EVEN DO?
OKAY, SO... MAYBE THERE WAS SOME TRUTH BEHIND THAT STORY OF MY BANISHMENT...
PERHAPS BLOWING AWAY THOSE GUARDS WITH FORBIDDEN MAGIC WHEN WE CROSSED THAT SECURITY CHECKPOINT WASN'T THE BEST IDEA...
THEY'RE ABOUT READY TO THROW THE BOOK AT YOU!
NOTHING GOOD WILL COME OF US STAYING HERE.
LET'S HIT THE ROAD, PETER GRILL!
RMB
RMB
R- RIGHT...
RMB
At that moment...

The bodacious bouncing of Peter Grill's babes' breasts...
RUMMMMMBBBBBBLLLEEEE...
ゴロゴロゴロ...
finally made their way to the Elven Village, and manifested heavy rain clouds in the sky above.
For the more scientific minded among you, here's how these events came to be.
The jiggling of boobs caused a breeze in the air. The breeze in the air surprised the insects nearby. The surprised insects gobbled up the local supply of grain. The serious grain shortage caused an increase in the fishing of flying murder tuna. The decrease in flying murder tuna fish numbers caused their natural prey, the sharks, to become more active, and they formed a sharknado. The sharknado caused rain clouds to form over the Elven Village.
Even incredibly small movements like the jiggling of boobs can set in motion a chain of cause and effect...
that can have a huge impact on the world as a whole.
This would eventually come to be known as the "Balloon-breast Effect"!

The heavy droplets of rain that came pouring down on the village...

would seem unremarkable to anyone at first glance.

But for the three-thousandfold more sensitive man Peter Grill, this rain was no laughing matter!

FSHHHHHHH

Ahhaaaaahnnn♥!!

He climaxed furiously with every droplet that stuck his chiseled form!
Furthermore, in their attempt to escape into the eaves of a tree, the two found themselves deep in the den of an ivy tentacle slime!

Desperate and panicking, Vegan tried to offer up Peter Grill as a sacrifice to the creature in her stead, but he caught her by the ankle, foiling her plan in a grand manner!

Pitifully, they mutually dragged each other down to their shared doom...
and after the creature had its fun toying with them, the two were left exhausted.

To evade their pursuers' eyes and get some rest...
they found themselves a conveniently hollow tree trunk and took shelter within.
WAAAAHHH!
WILLYA PLEASE JUST DO SOMETHING ABOUT MY BODY ALREADY?!
NO WAY AM I ESCAPING LIKE THIS!
HMM...
THIS SYMBOL APPEARS TO BE THE FORBIDDEN "SENSITIVE" SPELL.
GUESS SHE MASTERED THAT TOO, HUH?
I SEE...
SO THAT'S WHY YOU'VE BEEN AS HARD AS MATH THIS ENTIRE TIME!

POKE POKE, POKE, POOOOKE.
SMOOSH
SMOOSH
SMOOSH
QUIT !!!!!!!T!
IT'S NOT A TOY Y'KNOW?!
※ The sound of something incredible going on down there.
HEH HEH HEH...
BUT HOW UTTERLY CONVENIENT FOR ME...
TWITCH
FFT...
IF YOU WERE TO ASK ME TO FREE YOU FROM THAT CURSE...
DROP...
WHATEVER COULD I ASK FOR IN EXCHANGE?

THOUGH I SUSPECT YOU ALREADY KNOW, DON'T YOU?
EH, PETER GRILL...!

チュン
CHIRP
チュン
CHIRP
チュン
CHIRP
チュン
CHIRP
IT ALWAYS ENDS UP THIS WAY...
IT'S LIKE A QUOTA AT THIS POINT.
YOU WERE RAVENOUS LAST NIGHT...

IT FEELS GOOD...
TO BE SO *DESIRED* BY YOU.
RRRRR
HAVE YOU HAD YOUR FILL...?!
WE NEED TO GET OUR ASSES BACK TO PANNA COTTA, SO MAKE WITH THE COUNTERSPELL ALREADY!
YEAAAH, 'BOUT THAT...
THING IS...
IT'S BEYOND MY ABILITIES.

THESE "SENSITIVITY RAISING" SPELLS ARE SIMILAR TO THE "ERECTION MAINTAINING" SPELL I USED ON YOU. ONLY THE CASTERS THEMSELVES CAN DISPEL IT.
WAIT, WAIT, WAIT!
SO, WHY'D WE END UP BONING AGAIN?!
HEH.
NOW, I NEVER SAID *I'D* BE THE ONE LIFTING THE CURSE, DID I?
YOUUUUUU!!
BUT THAT MEANS...
WE NEED TO GO BACK AND TRACK DOWN FULLTALIA TO REMOVE THE CURSE!
IF WE LEAVE THE VILLAGE NOW, I'LL BE MISTER THREE THOUSAND FOR THE REST OF MY FREAKIN' LIFE!
YEAH, THAT ACTUALLY WORKS OUT GREAT FOR ME, SO...
TREMBL
TREMBL
TREMBL
STOP TALKING LIKE THIS *ISN'T* YOUR PROB-LEM...!

JEEZ, CAN'T RELY ON HER AFTER ALL...
I NEED TO CARVE MY OWN PATH SOMEHOW...!
LET'S THINK LOGICALLY HERE. WHAT'S MY NEXT MOVE?
CRAWLING BACK TO THE MANSION IS OUT OF THE QUESTION.
THEY'D LOCK ME UP AGAIN AND I'D BE BACK TO SQUARE ONE.
AM I COMPLETELY SCREWED HERE?
IS THERE ANYTHING I PICKED UP ON THAT COULD BE OF ANY HELP IN THIS SITUA--
AH!!
COME TO THINK OF IT...
As the story goes, the door shall only open once they work together and pour magic into it.
You mean if Fulltalia and Vegan made up, they'd get whatever inheritance is in this store-house...?
Yeah...

Our immediate financial problems would be over...
and they might even be freed from their roles as ambassadors.
THAT'S IT!
IF I SOLVE FULLTALIA'S FINANCIAL PROBLEMS, THERE'LL BE NO NEED FOR HER TO BE THE SPECIAL GOODWILL AMBASSADOR FOR THE VILLAGE ANYMORE!
THEN SHE'LL HAVE NO REASON TO OBSESS OVER MY BABY GRAVY AND SHOULD DISPEL THIS CURSE FOR ME!
THAT WON'T SOLVE THE PROBLEM OF THE ELVES HUNTING ME DOWN, BUT I'LL TAKE IT!
※ The butt of a man who excels in short-term fixes.
BUT...
I DON'T KNOW ENOUGH ABOUT THOSE TWO TO FIX THEIR FAMILIAL SQUABBLES.
FIRST, I NEED TO GET THE DOWN-LOW ABOUT WHAT HAPPENED BETWEEN THEM...
AND THERE'S NO TIME FOR SUBTLETY!
I'M GOING TO USE YOUR GULLIBILITY AGAINST YOU!
GLARE

WHOMP!!
WH...!
WHAT'S GOTTEN INTO YOU?!
TELL ME...
HUH?!
WHY DID THE HOUSE OF ELDORIEL FALL INTO RUIN?
WHY DID YOU CONCEAL YOUR IDENTITY TO COME IN SEARCH OF MY MAN BREW...?
AS THE MAN WHO WILL ONE DAY BE YOUR HUS-BAND...
FTT
I...

I WISH TO KNOW...
EVERY LAST THING ABOUT YOU...!
WHAA...?
B'BMP...

FIRST, I NEED TO FIND OUT WHAT CAUSED THE FEUD BETWEEN THEM...
AND THEN HAVE THEM COOPERATE IN GETTING THAT STOREHOUSE OPEN.
SO IN THE END...
WE CAN GET AT THE "INHERITANCE"...
THAT LIES WITHIN!
Chapter 30 / END

PETER GRILL
AND THE PHILOSOPHER'S TIME

Previously, on *Peter Grill*...

I WISH TO KNOW...
EVERY LAST THING ABOUT YOU...!
WHAAA...?
B'BMP...
Chapter 31 Peter Grill and the Trick to Apologizing

FIRST, I NEED TO FIND OUT WHAT CAUSED THE RIFT BETWEEN THEM, FIX IT...
AND THEN HAVE THEM OPEN THAT STOREHOUSE SO THEY CAN GET THEIR INHERI-TANCE...!
THIS IS THE MISSION THAT HAS BEEN THRUST UPON ME!
JEEZ...
WHY DO YOU WANT TO GET INTO ALL THAT STUFF FOR?
TALK ABOUT YOUR WEIRD INTER-ESTS...
WELL, IF I MUST...
I SUPPOSE THERE'S NO CHOICE IN THE MATTER.
GREAT!
GULLIBLE AS EVER!
SNAP
FFFSHINK
!!

AS I RECALL...
ROUGHLY THREE YEARS AGO, I HAD EATEN FULLTALIA'S PUDDING, WHICH BROUGHT ABOUT A... MINOR ARGUMENT.
DAY AFTER DAY SHE WOULD SHRIEK ABOUT "MY PUDDING" THIS AND "MY PUDDING" THAT!
SHE'S TRULY A SMALL-MINDED INDIVIDUAL. THOUGH I ADMIT THERE MAY HAVE BEEN A MINISCULE AMOUNT OF GUILT ON MY PART...
I COULDN'T JUST UP AND APOLOGIZE TO HER... I MEAN, C'MON...
SO, I DEVISED A PLAN TO RETURN HER LOST PUDDING BY USING THE FORBIDDEN MAGIC SEALED DEEP WITHIN THE VILLAGE'S LABYRINTH.
I DON'T THINK I'VE EVER SEEN YOU NOT USE FORBIDDEN MAGIC...

KRAKK
UNNHH!!
KRIKK
—HOWEVER...
IT'S NO USE, I CAN'T CONTAIN IT...!
THE PUD-DING...
THE PUD-DING IS OUT OF CON-TROL!
THE VILLAGE ENDED UP BURIED IN PUDDING, AND IT TOOK MONTHS FOR US TO REBUILD.
THE HOUSE OF ELDORIEL WAS FORCED TO FRONT UP FOR ALL DAMAGES...
THIS IS WHAT LED TO THE "MINESTRONE IN THE PUDDING INCIDENT"!

AND THAT'S WHY THEY BANISHED YOU FROM THE VILLAGE?
HMPH!!
YOU'RE A PER-CEPTIVE ONE.
RIGHT...
NOW, I GET IT...
SHE'S WORSE THAN I DARED IMAGINE...
I CAN'T SEE A SINGLE WAY TO DEFEND HER! COMPLETELY IRREDEEMABLE!
I ALWAYS KNEW YOU WERE A HOPELESS CASE, YOU KNOW, BUT...
YOU KEEP FINDING WAYS TO EXCEED MY EXPECTATIONS. IT'S IMPRESSIVE, REALLY.
AND WHAT'S THAT SUPPOSED TO MEAN?!

WELL, ANY-WAY...
I UNDER-STAND WHAT YOU DID TO THE VILLAGE NOW.
BUT...
THERE'S STILL ONE THING I DON'T GET.
ANSWER ME THIS!
WHY DID YOU...
PRETEND TO BE THE SPECIAL GOODWILL AMBASSA-DOR, AND COME TO CLAIM MY STALLION SAUCE?!
......
NOT TELLIN'!
POUT
YOU LITTLE...!
YOU CAN FREELY TALK ABOUT CAUSING THE PUDDINGPOCALYPSE BUT SOMEHOW THIS IS A BRIDGE TOO FAR?!

VEGAN! YOU ARE AWARE THAT I MAY BE YOUR HUSBAND ONE DAY?!
I DON'T WANT OUR RELATIONSHIP GETTING OFF ON THE WRONG FOOT!
I WANT US TO BE OPEN ABOUT EVERYTHING!
UHN...
NHH...!!
GHHK...
I'VE...
ALWAYS REGRETTED...
THE FACT THAT I...
WAS UNABLE TO APOLOGIZE TO HER.
NOT EVEN ONCE...
FOR THE PUDDING...
AND FOR THE DOWNFALL OF OUR HOUSE.

I'M ALWAYS LIKE THIS...
I JUST... CAN'T BE HONEST.
LEAST OF ALL WITH HER...
SO, WHEN THE SENATE APPROVED PROJECT SUPER ELF...
AND IT WAS CLEAR FULLTALIA, WITH BLESSED PHYSIQUE AND LOW STANDING...
WAS GOING TO BE FORCED INTO THE UNENVIABLE POSITION OF SPECIAL GOODWILL AMBASSA-DOR...

I FELT IT WAS ONLY FAIR THAT I SHOULDER THAT BURDEN FOR HER.
ANY-THING TO...
I TOOK THE POSITION IN HER STEAD.
LIGHTEN HER LOAD.

HUH...?
BUT THAT MEANS...
SHE CAME TO ME TO SACRIFICE HERSELF...
FOR FULLTALIA'S SAKE...?
I THOUGHT SHE WAS AN ARROGANT, WORTHLESS, SELFISH, RACIST, HORRIBLY INCONSIDERATE BOWL OF BUBBLING RAPIST, BUT...
MAYBE SHE'S NOT SO BAD AFTER ALL...
※ Similar phenomenon to when a bad guy occasionally does one tiny act of good and it dramatically increases his likeability.

BUT THEN THAT MEANS...
THE PROBLEM IS THAT VEGAN ISN'T BEING HONEST WITH FULLTALIA. IT'S NOT LIKE SHE HATES HER WITH A PASSION OR ANYTHING...
THEN...
IN ORDER TO RESTORE THEIR RELATIONSHIP, WE NEED TO...
LET'S GO BACK TO THE MANSION!
HUUUH?
ARE YOU OFF YOUR ROCKER?
THOSE THINGS YOU JUST SAID TO ME...

YOU'RE GOING TO TELL THEM RIGHT TO FULLTALIA'S FACE!
IF YOU CAN HONESTLY EXPRESS YOUR FEELINGS TO HER, I'M SURE SHE'LL UNDERSTAND!
IF I WAS ABLE TO DO THAT, THIS WOULDN'T BE SO DIFFICULT, YOU FECKLESS JACKA-NAPE!
DRAGON PUNCH!
I'M THE ELDEST DAUGHTER OF THE NOBLE HOUSE OF ELDORIEL!
MY PRIDE WOULD *NEVER* ALLOW ME TO BOW MY HEAD TO MY YOUNGER SISTER!
THIS IS NO TIME TO BE THINK-ING ABOUT PRIDE!
FLASH!!
!!

DON'T WANNA, DON'T WANNA, DON'T WANNAAA-AAH!
JUH
JUH
JUH
JAB!!
DON'T YOU BE THROWING A TAN-TRUM!
WHAT ARE YOU, FIVE YEARS OLD?!
DON'T WANNAAAAAAAA!
HOW OLD ARE YOU, JEEZ...!
LISTEN TO ME!
NAB
I KNOW THAT DEEP DOWN, YOU WANT TO APOLOGIZE TO FULLTALIA AND GET THIS OVER WITH...!
THE ONLY PROBLEM IS HOW YOU EXPRESS THOSE FEELINGS TO HER!

FOLLOW MY LEAD, AND I'M SURE YOU'LL COME TO AN UNDERSTANDING!
TRUST ME, VEGAN!
NH...
NHH...
AND WHILE WE'RE ON THE SUBJECT...
THERE'S A BETTER WAY OF FREEING FULLTALIA FROM HER FATE WITHOUT DRAINING ME OF MY GROIN GOOP!
WH... WHAT WAS THAT?!
DON'T YOU REMEMBER THAT STOREHOUSE YOUR GREAT-GREAT-GRANDFATHER LEFT YOU?
IF YOU CAN BOTH WORK TOGETHER LONG ENOUGH, THE "INHERITANCE" CONTAINED WITHIN'LL SOLVE ALL YOUR PROBLEMS!

THAT'S FAR ENOUGH, YOU!
BAM!!
HEH HEH HEH...
DO FORGIVE US, VEGAN-SAMA.
GH!!
BUT NOBODY DISOBEYS FULLTALIA-SAMA...
COME NOW! BACK TO THE MANSION WITH YOU, PETER-DONO!
HUP
SHPP
GAAAAHH!

WATCH ITTTT!
WE'RE DONE RUNNING AND HIDING!
?!
TH-THAT'S GONNA BREAK!
SAY WHAT?!
WE'RE GOING BACK TO THE MANSION...
WHERE YOU'LL BE CONFRONTING YOUR CRIMES, VEGAN!

WHSHHHH
HFF! HFF!
THIS IS NOT THE WAY I EXPECTED THE WINDS TO BE BLOWING...
TO THINK YOU WOULD RETURN TO ME OF YOUR OWN ACCORD...!

STILL...
BEFORE WE BEGIN...
PERCHANCE MIGHT YOU DISPEL THIS THREE THOUSAND TIMES SENSITIVITY SPELL.
I'M DOING MY BEST TO STAY UNDER CONTROL, BUT I'M A GENTLE BREEZE AWAY FROM DROWNING THIS ROOM IN LOVE JUICE!
FIDJIT
FIDJIT
WAIT...
FIRST, JUST... LISTEN TO WHAT VEGAN HAS TO SAY!
SILENCE!
I HAVE NOTHING TO SAY TO A BANISHED HERETIC!
SNAP
GH...
PLEASE...
SO MUCH FOR COMPLIANCE...
WE'RE CURRENTLY BOTH "SENSITIVE" AREN'T WE?
THAT PUTS US IN THE SAME BOAT!!
MAIN-TAINING THIS CON-FRONTATION WILL ONLY DESTROY US BOTH!
AND IT SEEMS...
YOU THINK YOUR SPECIAL GOODWILL AMBASSADOR POSITION HAS TO BE CARRIED THROUGH TO THE END, BUT...

YOU'RE MAKING A BIG MISTAKE!
?!
THERE IS A BETTER WAY TO RESOLVE THIS SITUA-TION!
ONE WE'LL DEMON-STRATE RIGHT NOW!
COME ON, VEGAN!
STIP
DO IT, JUST LIKE I TOLD YOU!
YOU CAN DO THIS. I BELIEVE IN YOU!

Listen up, Vegan.
It's not just the words you speak that matter. Your expression, attitude, and body language all fall under the umbrella of "nonverbal communication."
If your pride keeps you from saying the words that need to come out, do the following!
Instead of saying it, show her with your body language and the look on your face!
First up, the expression!
SNAP
An apology has to have a sincere expression to go alongside it!
Even if you don't mean a word you're saying, just make sure to have a pensive, meek, nervous and pathetic look on your face the entire time!

I've literally never bowed my head to anyone before. I'm not even sure how that's supposed to look.
Hmm...
since you need a simple example...
Imagine the expression you'd make if you found a poor abandoned and hurt widdle kitty on the road.
MEWWW!
Your expression must be one of deep complexity! Of love, pity and the aching of your heart all mixed into one! Such is the nature of apologizing!
HM...
A CAT, HUH...?
SUH...
SIS-TER...?
UH...!
TH...
THAT EXPRES-SION...!

?!
WH-WHAT IS SHE CONVEYING EXACTLY...?
BUH...?
I CAN'T READ IT AT ALL...!
NOT ONE BIT!
RUMMMMMMBBBBLLLLLLEEE...
WHAT IS SHE EVEN...?!

SHOOOP...
?!

SHE REALLY DOESN'T WANT TO LOWER HER HEAD, DOES SHE...?
I SEE...
I UNDER-STAND YOU COMPLETELY, SIS.
Y-YOU DO?!

DOOM
DOOM
DOOM
NOOOO...
POP
POP
POP
TREMBL
TREMBL
THIS MEANS WAR, DOESN'T IT?!
DOOM
DOOM
IS THAT HOW I'M MEANT TO UNDERSTAND YOU?
SHE DIDN'T UNDER-STAND ONE BIT!
HMPH? I'M NOT GETTING THROUGH TO HER, AM I?
NAH...
SHE READ YOUR STUPIDITY LOUD AND CLEAR!
THEN I GROW WEARY OF THIS TIRESOME FARCE!
SNAP
TIME TO SETTLE THIS WITH MY OWN TWO HANDS!

WE SISTERS HAVE NEVER NEEDED WORDS TO COMMUNICATE...
HAVE WE?
FULL-TALIA!
YES... YOU'RE RIGHT, SISTER DEAR...
ON THAT I WHOLE-HEARTEDLY AGREE.
WE HAVE OUR OWN WAY OF DOING THINGS.

THE LAST ONE LEFT STANDING...
CLAIMS THE RIGHT TO TAKE PETER GRILL TO POUND TOWN AS SPECIAL GOODWILL AMBASSADOR...!
B-BMP
B-BMP
B-BMP
B-BMP
B-BMP
B-BMP
In the end, they resort to violence!
They'll resolve this the only way they know how!
VS
Chapter 31 / END

PETER GRILL
AND THE PHILOSOPHER'S TIME

THE LAST ONE LEFT STANDING...
ドド
B-BMP
ドド
B-BMP
ドド
B-BMP
CLAIMS THE RIGHT TO TAKE PETER GRILL TO POUND TOWN AS SPECIAL GOODWILL AMBASSADOR...!
ドド
B-BMP
ドド
B-BMP
ドド
B-BMP
In the end, they resort to violence!
They'll resolve this the only way they know how!
VS
Chapter 32 Peter Grill and the Golden Inheritance

WHOOSH
!!
YOU IGNORAMUS!
BE A GOOD LITTLE SISTER FOR ONCE AND DO AS I SAY!
WHAT ARE YOU ON ABOUT?! I'LL *REMIND* YOU THAT YOU DESTROYED OUR HOUSE AND WERE BANISHED FROM THE VILLAGE AS A HERETIC!
TIME TO DELIVER THAT CORKSCREW BLOW TO THAT STUPID FACE OF YOURS I'VE BEEN PROMISING!

HYAH!
WOOOSHH
YIKES!!
WHUD BOOOOM
The forbidden magic unleashed by the sisters' death match caused so much damage to the surrounding area that it could only be described as disastrous!

The Elven Senate House exploded!
LAZY SON OF A SENATOOOOR!
The lazy son of that senator was forced into an early (and permanent) retirement!
The ancient poplar tree, estimated to be one hundred million years old, went up in flames!
POPLAAAAAR!
The Elven Village was thrown into utter confusion and panic!
PANIC!
CONFUSION!

WHUDD SMAKK...
BOOM BOOM...
......
DEEEEEEFINITELY GETTING BANISHED FOR THIS...
NO WAY CAN I HELP THEM NOW.
WH-WHAT'S GOING ON?!
BRAS-SALIA-SAMA...!
Y-YOU SEE... FIRST THIS... THEN THIS...
AHH...!
MORE DAMAGES TO PAY...
FAINT...
BRAS-SALIA-SAMA!
HEY, PETER-SAMA.
THINK YOU COULD MANAGE TRYING TO GET THEM TO STOP DESTROYING THE VILLAGE?
EHH...
YOU'RE ASKING THE THREE-THOU-SAND-TIMES-MORE-SENSITIVE MAN?

WE CAN FIX THAT FOR YOU, Y'KNOW ...
HUH?!
YOU CAN LIFT THE CURSE?!
BEST WE CAN FIGURE, IF YOU GOBBLE DOWN THREE KILOGRAMS OF THESE TRANQUILIZING HERBS, YOU'LL BE GOOD TO GO.
でんっ!!
TA DAA!!
Weeds growing nearby.
THAT'S THE STUPIDEST THING I'VE EVER HEARD!
RIGHT, LET'S STUFF 'EM DOWN HIS CRAW!
C'MON, C'MON, C'MON!
KNOCK IT OFF! NO WAY AM I EATING ALL THOSE HERBS!
HUMANS DON'T HAVE THE RIGHT BACTERIA IN THEIR STOMACHS TO BREAK DOWN THAT MANY PLANT FIBERS THE SAME WAY ELVES D--
※ Fun fact.
GRMAHHH?!
AH!
AH!
HAAH.
HAAH.
HAAH.

WHAT'S THE MATTER?
MOVING QUITE A BIT SLOWER THAN USUAL, AREN'T YOU, FULLTALIA?!
HAAH.
HAAH.
MM-HMMM...
OH, IT'S BECAUSE YOU'RE THREE THOUSAND TIMES MORE SENSITIVE THAN NORMAL! NOW I REMEMBER...
OH MY, HAVE YOU BEEN CREAMING YOUR PANTIES THIS WHOLE FIGHT?
GH...!
C'MON THEN, WHAT'S WRONG?
COME AT ME, SIS!
WOOBLE
WOBBLE
WOOB
Y...YOU TRULY HAVE THE PERSONALITY OF A DIRTY PUDDLE OF FILTH...!
IT MAKES ME SICK TO THINK THAT THE SAME BLOOD FLOWS THROUGH OUR VEINS!

HMPH!!
I HOPE IT'S FINALLY CLEAR TO YOU NOW!
NO YOUNGER SISTER CAN EVER BEST HER ELDER...
YOU'D BEST GIVE UP NOW AND LEAVE THE POSITION OF SPECIAL GOODWILL AMBASSADOR TO ME!
H-HOW COULD I...?!
YOU WERE BANISHED FROM THE VILLAGE, CAST OUT! I COULD NEVER ENTRUST THE POSITION TO YOU!
HMPH...
IT'S CLEAR THAT EVERYONE IN THE SENATE IS TRYING TO PUNISH US BY FORCING THAT HUMAN'S BLOOD UPON US!
SO LONG AS I'M THE ONE TO BEAR THE BURDEN OF PUNISHMENT...
THAT SHOULD SATIATE THEIR WRATH.

YOU...
WHY ARE YOU ALWAYS LIKE THIS...?!
GRTT...
ALWAYS SO ARROGANT...!
ALWAYS DECIDING...
EVERY-THING!
ON YOUR OWWWW-WWN!
FLASH
Minestrone Defense Force Third Battalion **Pizza Mozzarella** High Elf (♂) 339 years old
OH MY...
IT GAVE ME QUITE THE SHOCK!
Here is how he would later describe the fight, as a close witness to the events that day.

ALL THESE FORBIDDEN NUCLEAR TYPE SPELLS STARTED MAKING THIS DREADFUL DIN FROM THE MIDDLE OF TOWN!
I MEAN... HERE, OF ALL PLACES? WHAT A COMPLETE LACK OF COMMON SENSE...
HA HA...!
EH?
THOSE TWO WERE SIS-TERS?
MY, NO... THAT SIMPLY COULDN'T BE!
WHY, THOSE TWO MANIACS WERE OUT FOR EACH OTHER'S BLOOD!
IT WAS PROBABLY ONLY ONE OR TWO MINUTES...
THEY WERE CASTING THESE BLASPHEMOUS CURSES, FORBIDDEN ONES THAT I COULD BARELY EVEN DESCRIBE SWIRLING AROUND THEM...
TO BE HONEST, I THOUGHT I'D DIED ALREADY...

SUDDENLY, THE SMALL ONE STARTED BUILDING UP THIS ALL-ENCOMPASSING BALL OF MAGIC, YOU SEE...
"GOOD GRACIOUS, SHE'S A GONER!"
WHEN OUT OF NO-WHERE...
I THOUGHT TO MYSELF.

IT WAS AN IMPECCABLE ROUNDHOUSE BLOCK. I WAS LEFT AGHAST!
WITH BUT A MOVEMENT, HE DEFLECTED IT, SENT IT SPIRALING INTO THE AIR!

WHAT'S THAT?
THE STRONGEST MAN ON EARTH?
HA HAH...
I SEE, SO THAT WAS HIM.
BUT NOW THAT YOU MENTION IT, IT ALL MAKES SENSE.
THAT MAN WAS INCREDIBLE.
HA HAH...
THAT'S *ENOUGH*, YOU TWO...
I'LL HANDLE THIS FIGHT OF YOURS!
DON'T INTERFERE, PETER GRILL!
THIS IS THE *ONLY WAY* THAT FULLTALIA WILL UNDERSTAND!
SHE'S RIGHT.
THIS IS A MATTER BETWEEN SISTERS!
STOP! THERE'S NO NEED TO KEEP FIGHTING! ALL OF THIS IS FUTILE!

......
YOU CAN'T FORGIVE VEGAN. CAN YOU, FULLTALIA?
O-OF COURSE I CAN'T...
HAVE YOU ANY INKLING OF THE UTTER HELL THAT PUDDING INCIDENT SHE CAUSED WROUGHT UPON ME...?!
IT'S *ALWAYS* THE SAME...
SHE JUST GOES CHARGING IN HEAD-ON, CREATES A BLUNDER AND NEVER OWNS UP TO IT...!
SHE NEVER APOLO-GIZES! NOT ONCE!
I KNOW HOW YOU FEEL...!
SHE'S WORTHLESS! WORSE THAN A STICKY PUDDLE OF FILTH CIRCLING A DRAIN!
POINT
BUT I KNOW...

THAT WHILE SHE'S A LITTLE CLUMSY...
DEEP DOWN SHE'S TRULY SORRY FOR WHAT SHE DID!
AM I EXPECTED TO BELIEVE THAT?!
THINK BACK...
THE WHOLE MINESTRONE IN THE PUDDING INCIDENT ONLY HAPPENED BECAUSE SHE WANTED TO GIVE YOU BACK YOUR PUDDING!
THE REASON SHE CAME TO ME, IS...
SHE WANTED TO SACRIFICE HERSELF FOR YOU...!
TO BEAR MY CHILDREN IN YOUR PLACE!

TMP...
TH-THAT CAN'T BE...!
INCONCEIVABLE!
SHE WOULDN'T ...!
SHE WOULD NEVER...
DO ANYTHING FOR ANYONE...!
BEING UNABLE TO REPENT WITH WORDS, SHE CHOSE TO SHOW YOU HOW SHE FELT WITH ACTIONS INSTEAD!
BUT STILL! I UNDERSTAND WHY THAT'S HARD FOR YOU TO ACCEPT!
VEGAN!
TWITCH
IT'S TIME!
IT'S TIME TO TELL HER!

JUST ONE WORD...!
ONE WORD IS ENOUGH!
BE HONEST...
AND TELL HER HOW YOU *TRULY* FEEL!
FTT
VE- GAN...!
IS THAT YOU, VEGAN...?!

GH...
GRAND-MOTHER...!
YES...! PERFECT TIMING!
ALL ACCORDING TO PLAN!
TAP...
COME NOW, VEGAN...
YOU DON'T WANT...
TO MAKE YOUR GRANDMOTHER SUFFER ANY MORE, DO YOU...?
I...

I...
MY
BAD.
IT
WAS
MY
FAULT.
THE
PUDDING...
THE
FALL
OF
OUR
HOUSE...
ALL
OF
IT...
IT
WAS
ALL
ME.
PLEASE
FORGIVE
ME...
FULL-
TALIA...!

RAISE YOUR HEAD...
MY DEAR SISTER.
FU...
FULL-TALIA...!

THIS AIN'T SOMETHING YOU CAN JUST FREAKING APOLOGIZE AWAY!
PAMMO
ばごん

WHU!!
PGGHH!
PYAAAH!
ぎゅるるるああッ!!
WHU WHU WHU WHU
WHOOSHH!!
A CORKSCREW BLOW!
FLAW-LESSLY EXE-CUTED!

ONE WORD DOESN'T MAKE EVERYTHING JUST GO AWAY.
HOW-EVER...
FOR THE FIRST TIME...
YOU'VE ADMITTED YOU DID SOMETHING WRONG.
THAT ONE PUNCH CAN'T PUT EVERYTHING RIGHT ON ITS OWN EITHER.
BUT IT DID...
FEEL QUITE SATISFY-ING.
H-HMPH...!

VEGAN...
FULL-TALIA...
GRAND-MOTHER...
SHE'S YOUR SISTER...
YOUR ONLY SISTER.
YOU HAVE TO...
GET ALONG...
THAT'S THE END OF THIS STORY.
WELL, I SAY THAT, BUT...
WE AREN'T DONE YET.

THERE'S STILL ONE THING...
LEFT TO DO, RIGHT?
FULL-TALIA...
WE HAVE TO POUR OUR MAGIC IN AT THE SAME TIME!
YES...
DON'T MESS IT UP!
DWOOOOOSHH!!
FINAL-LY...
ONCE THEY GET THE INHERITANCE THAT'S LOCKED UP IN HERE, THEY CAN QUIT BEING SPECIAL GOODWILL AMBASSADORS FOR THE VILLAGE.
I GUESS THIS MEANS...
GOODBYE TO VEGAN, AS WELL.

RMB
WHOA...
RMB!!
ALL RIGHT...!!
LET'S GO...
CLAIM THAT INHERITANCE!

FSHHHHHH
NHH?
THE ROOTS ARE EVEN GROWING IN HERE!
WHERE IS IT?!
WHERE'S THE INHERITANCE?!
PETER GRILL, OVER THERE!

KRIKK
KRAKK
SNAPP
OOM
YOU DID WELL TO MAKE IT HERE...
V-W-H-O-O-S-H...
!!
YOU'RE...
VEGETALIA-SAMA! GRANDFATHER!
VEGAN...
FULLTALIA...

I'M OVER-JOYED.
YOU HAVE FINALLY OPENED THIS STOREHOUSE AND MADE YOUR WAY INSIDE.
SOME KIND OF MAGICAL RECORD...
HUNH, HE WAS MESSING AROUND WITH FANCY MAGIC LIKE THIS BEFORE HE DIED...
YOU HAVE ALWAYS HAD AN ASTONISH-INGLY TERRIBLE RELATION-SHIP.
WITH YOUR PERSON-ALITIES, AND THE QUALITIES YOU WERE BLESSED WITH, WE COULD NOT EASILY RECTIFY THIS.
AND SO, I DECIDED TO LEAVE YOU THIS STOREHOUSE, CONTAINING THE VALUED "INHERITANCE" OF THE HOUSE OF ELDORIEL.
TOWARD A COMMON GOAL, I THOUGHT PERHAPS YOU MIGHT COOPERATE SOMEDAY...
JUST A BIT OF FUN, I SUPPOSE, CROSSING MY FINGERS THAT SOMEDAY YOU MIGHT ACTUALLY SUCCEED.

BE-
HOLD.
FTT...
THESE TWO ARROWS.
HMPH!!
SNAPP
TRY TO SNAP THESE TWO ARROWS TOGETHER, AND THEY WILL BREAK...
BUT THEY *HAVE* BECOME A LITTLE MORE DIFFICULT TO BREAK, NO?
IF YOU WORK TOGETHER AS A FAMILY WITH A SHARED PURPOSE, YOU WILL SURELY BE ABLE TO OVERCOME WHATEVER OBSTACLES LIFE PLACES IN YOUR WAY.
THAT IS THE "INHERITANCE" I MEAN TO GIVE TO YOU.
YOUR TEAM-WORK.
THE CONSIDERATE WAY IN WHICH YOU HELP EACH OTHER.
TWITCH
Y-YOU'RE FREAKIN' KIDDIN' ME?!
DON'T TELL ME THE INHERITANCE IS...?!

THAT'S IT!
YOUR INHERITANCE IS...
PROOF OF YOUR MIGHTY SISTERLY BOND!
SHIIIIIIIINE

POP
POP
POP
SNAP
RAAAHHH!
GRAAAH! WHAT IS THE MEANING OF THIS?!
HAD YOU GONE COMPLETELY SENILE, GRAND-FATHER?!
WHO CARES ABOUT SOME STUPID BOND! GIVE US SOMETHING THAT'S ACTUALLY WORTH A DAMN, YA OLD GOAT!
RAAAHHH!
WHOP
WHOP
WHOP
WHOP
......
THIS HAS ALL...
GONE HORRIBLY WRONG!

WELP! ONLY ONE OPTION LEFT...
RUN AWAY BEFORE THEY TURN AROUND AND--
FTT——...
AND WHERE DO YOU THINK YOU'RE GOING, PETER GRILL?!
UHH?!
GULP
ゴゴゴゴゴゴゴゴ
RUUUUUM MMMMMB BB BLLL LE EEE E...
WAAH...
WAAAH...!!
S-STAY BACK, NOW!
I TRIED MY HARDEST! CAN I HELP IF THIS IS ALWAYS THE WAY THINGS END UP FOR ME?!
?
NOW THAT WE'VE DETERMINED THE INHERITANCE WE WERE LEFT HAS NO MONETARY VALUE...
YOU'LL UNDERSTAND WE'RE LEFT WITH LITTLE RECOURSE BUT TO ACT AS SPECIAL GOODWILL AMBASSADORS AND CONTINUE YOUR BLOODLINE.

YES...
ALL THAT FIGHTING HAS DOUBTLESS INCREASED THE DAMAGES WE'LL HAVE TO PAY BACK.
IN ORDER TO GET OURSELVES OUT OF THIS...
WE'LL HAVE TO *WORK TOGETHER*...
TO DOUBLE-TEAM YOU OUT OF MORE OF YOUR *PERSONAL PAN PUDDIN'* THAN EVER BEFORE!

The outskirts of the Elven Village.
WHOA, NELLY...
THAT WAS LIKE, SOOO CRAZY YOU GUYS!
I MUST ADMIT, I BELIEVED OUR BACON WAS COOKED WHEN THAT VOLCANO ERUPTED...
WHO WOULD'VE THOUGHT THAT CONVENIENTLY TIMED SHARKNADO WOULD WHISK US TO THE ELVEN VILLAGE IN RECORD TIME?!
ピコーン
BEEP
Powerful force detected.
BEEP
ピコーン
BEEP
ピコーン
SOUNDS LIKE PETER'S NEARBY, HUH.
WHOA...
THAT'S A REALLY CONVENIENT BEEP-Y THINGIE YOU GOT THERE, MISSLIM!

HE SHOULD BE SOME-WHERE AROUND HERE!
AH!
WHAT ABOUT INSIDE THAT STORE-HOUSE?!
SENPAI, SEN-PAAAI!
GUESS WHAT? WE'RE HERE TO SAVE Y--
チュン CHIRP
チュン CHIRP
チュン CHIRP
チュン CHIRP
NWHA?
チュン CHIRP
チュン CHIRP
チュン CHIRP
チュン CHIRP

CHIRP
CHIRP
CHIRP
CHIRP
CHIRP
MUH?

ゴゴゴゴ
RUMMMMMMM
WHAA?!
WHHA-HAAA-HAAAA--
AAAT ARE YOU GUYS DOING HERE?!
RUMBLLLLE
ゴゴゴ...
SENPAIII! DID YOU GIVE AWAY YOUR SPOOGE SAUCE TO ANOTHER WOMAN AGAIIIN?!
I-I'M JUST GLAD TO SEE YOU'RE SAFE, PETER-SAMA.
JEEZ! NOT MUCH ON RESTRAINT, ARE YOU?
I WAS EXPECTING IT, TO BE HONEST...
WAIT! LISTEN, THERE'S A REASON FOR ALL THIS I TELL YOU...
OUR FAMILY'S GETTING BIGGER AGAIN, YAAAAY!
Following this, as goes without saying, the treaty for regulating the distribution of Peter Grill's Pants Puddin' between different races was updated to include its newest member...

S-SISTER DEAR, WHO ARE ALL THESE PEOPLE...?
HMPH.
IT'S A LONG STORY.
How beautiful it is...
to have good friends.
GETTING ALONG WELL, AREN'T WE?

Mean-while...
in the fortress city of Panna Cotta, while Peter was away.
WE HAVE A WIN-NAH!
YOU'VE JUST WON A COUPLE'S TRIP ON OUR JOURNEY OF HOLY PILGRIMAGE!
CLANG
CLANG
CLANG
OOOOO
WOW, LUVELLIA-SAMA, THAT'S GREAT!
YEAH...
I NEVER DREAMED THAT I'D WIN...!

FATE PLAYED A HAND IN THIS, I KNOW IT.
PETER AND I...
WILL PRAY TOGETHER IN THE HOLY CITY OF EGG TART.
AND I'M SURE...
WE WILL BE BLESSED BY A BABY FROM THE MESSENGERS OF GOD, THE STORKS!
Chapter 32 / END

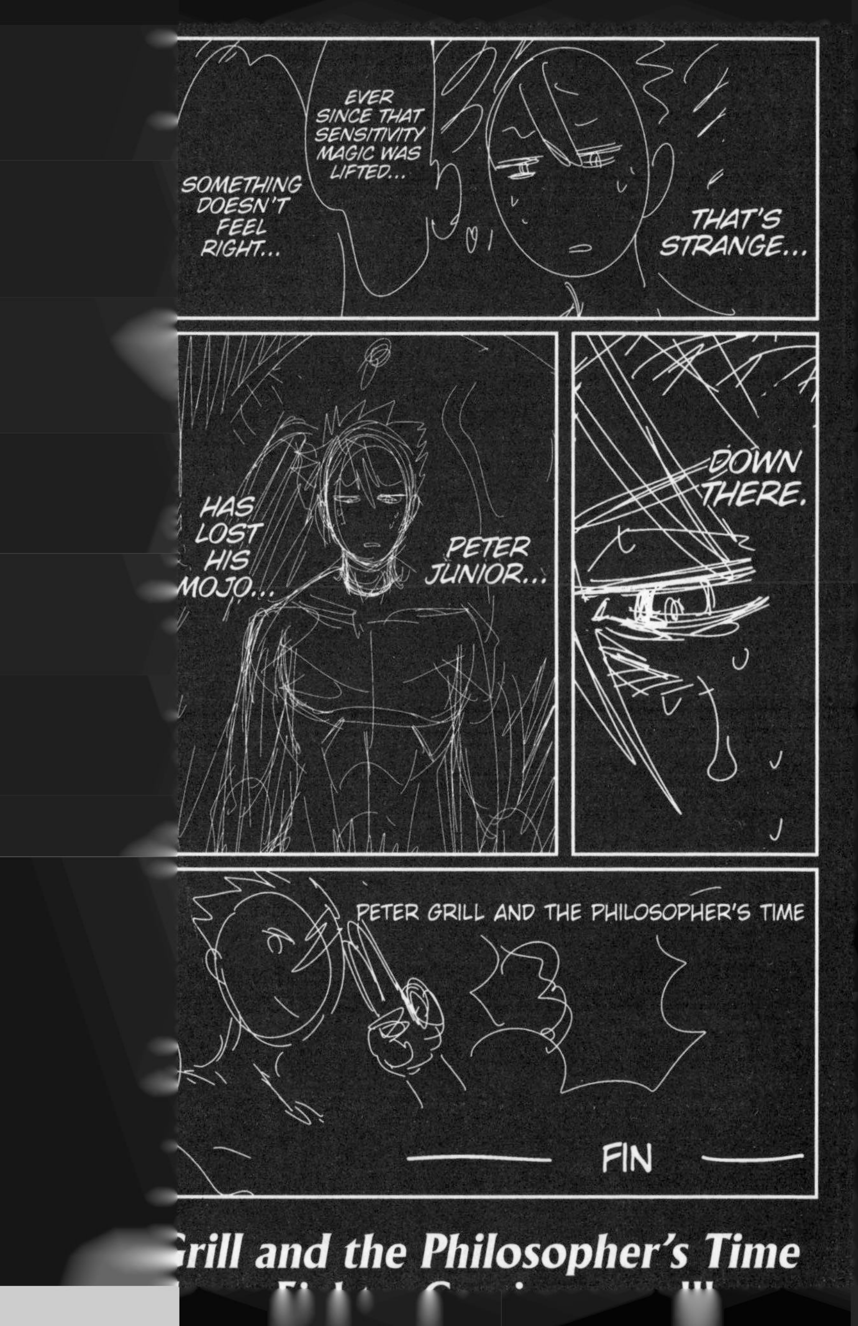
THAT'S STRANGE...
EVER SINCE THAT SENSITIVITY MAGIC WAS LIFTED...
SOMETHING DOESN'T FEEL RIGHT...
DOWN THERE.
PETER JUNIOR...
HAS LOST HIS MOJO...
PETER GRILL AND THE PHILOSOPHER'S TIME
FIN
rill and the Philosopher's Time

SEVEN SEAS' GHOST SHIP PRESENTS

story and art by **DAISUKE HIYAMA** **VOLUME 7**

TRANSLATION
Ben Trethewey

ADAPTATION
David Lumsdon

LETTERING
Mo Harrison

COVER AND LOGO DESIGN
Kris Aubin

PROOFREADER
Dawn Davis

EDITOR
Elise Kelsey

PREPRESS TECHNICIAN
Melanie Ujimori

PRINT MANAGER
Rhiannon Rasmussen-Silverstein

PRODUCTION MANAGER - GHOST SHIP
George Panella

PRODUCTION MANAGER
Lissa Pattillo

MANAGING EDITOR
Julie Davis

ASSOCIATE PUBLISHER
Adam Arnold

PUBLISHER
Jason DeAngelis

PETER GRILL AND THE PHILOSOPHER'S TIME VOL. 7

First published in Japan in 2017 by Futabasha Publishers Ltd., Tokyo.
English version published by Seven Seas Entertainment.
Under license from Futabasha Publishers Ltd.

ISBN: 978-1-63858-124-6
Printed in Canada
First Printing: February 2022
10 9 8 7 6 5 4 3 2 1

READING DIRECTIONS

This book reads from ***right to left***, Japanese style. If this is your first time reading manga, you start reading from the top right panel on each page and take it from there. If you get lost, just follow the numbered diagram here. It may seem backwards at first, but you'll get the hang of it! Have fun!!

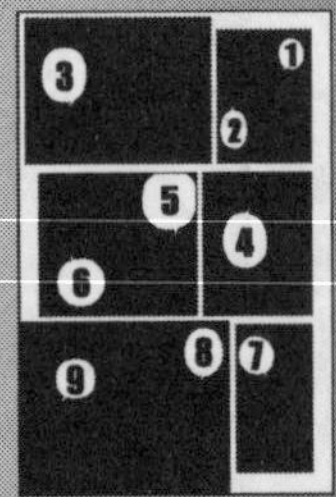